W9-DIU-996

The Minstrel in the Tower
Study Guide

by Rebecca Gilleland

Progeny Press

Limited permission to reproduce this study guide.

Purchase of this study guide entitles an individual teacher
to reproduce pages for use in the classroom or home.
Multiple teachers may not reproduce pages
from the same study guide.

The Minstrel in the Tower Study Guide
A Progeny Press Study Guide
by Rebecca Gilleland
with Andrew Clausen

Copyright © 1993 Progeny Press
All rights reserved.

Reproduction or translation of any part of this work
beyond that permitted by Section 107 or 108 of the
1976 United States Copyright Act without the written
permission of the copyright owner is unlawful.
Requests for permission or other information should be
addressed to Reprint Permissions, Progeny Press,
PO Box 100, Fall Creek, WI 54742-0100.

Printed in the United States of America.

ISBN 978-1-58609-306-8 Book
        978-1-58609-291-7 CD
        978-1-58609-397-6 Set

© 1993 Progeny Press

Table of Contents

Note to Instructor

How to Use Progeny Press Study Guides.   Progeny Press study guides are designed to help students better understand and enjoy literature by getting them to notice and understand how authors craft their stories and to show them how to think through the themes and ideas introduced in the stories. To properly work through a Progeny Press study guide, students should have easy access to a good dictionary, a thesaurus, a Bible (we use NIV translation, but that is up to your preference; just be aware of some differences in language), and sometimes a topical Bible or concordance. Supervised access to the Internet also can be helpful at times, as can a good set of encyclopedias.

Most middle grades and high school study guides take from eight to ten weeks to complete, generally working on one section per week. Over the years, we have found that it works best if the students completely read the novel the first week, while also working on a prereading activity chosen by the parent or teacher. Starting the second week, most parents and teachers have found it works best to work on one study guide page per day until the chapter sections are completed. Students should be allowed to complete questions by referring to the book; many questions require some cross-reference between elements of the stories.

Most study guides contain an Overview section that can be used as a final test, or it can be completed in the same way the chapter sections were completed. If you wish to perform a final test but your particular study guide does not have an Overview section, we suggest picking a couple of questions from each section of the study guide and using them as your final test.

Most study guides also have a final section of essays and postreading activities. These may be assigned at the parents' or teachers' discretion, but we suggest that students engage in several writing or other extra activities during the study of the novel to complement their reading and strengthen their writing skills.

As for high school credits, most Christian high schools with whom we have spoken have assigned a value of one-fourth credit to each study guide, and this also seems to be acceptable to colleges assessing homeschool transcripts.

Internet References

All websites listed in this study guide were checked for appropriateness at the time of publication. However, due to the changing nature of the Internet, we cannot guarantee that the URLs listed will remain appropriate or viable. Therefore, we urge parents and teachers to take care in and exercise careful oversight of their children's use of the Internet.

                    © 1993 Progeny Press

Synopsis

It is the year 1195. Roger and Alice live alone with their mother in a tiny cottage. Their father, a knight, left to fight in the Crusades five years earlier and never returned. Sick, feverish, and perhaps dreaming, their mother sends Roger and Alice on a journey to find an uncle they did not know they had. They carry with them their mother's lute. "Show him the eagle carved on the back," she tells her children. "Ask him to come quickly. Quickly!"

But on their journey they are kidnapped by two ruffians and locked in an old tower. With determination, Roger and Alice devise a plan for escape. Alice squeezes through a small window high in the tower and must continue the journey alone. Somehow, she must find her uncle and persuade him to help, and she no longer has the lute to prove her story.

Background Information

The Minstrel in the Tower is set in the year 1195 in Bordeaux, France, after the Third Crusade. The Crusades were Christian military battles to recapture the Holy Land, (Palestine, Israel, Jordan, Lebanon, and Syria) particularly Jerusalem, from the Moslems.

In 1187 the Turks captured the city of Jerusalem. This prompted many European rulers to begin the Third Crusade. Frederick I of Germany died before reaching the Holy Land. King Phillip II returned to France to plot against King Richard I (the Lion-Hearted) of England before the battles began.

King Richard, however, remained in the Holy Land and won several battles against Saladin, the Turkish leader. Richard did not retake Jerusalem, but he convinced the Turks to let Christian pilgrims go freely in and out of Jerusalem. The Third Crusade ended in 1192.

© 1993 Progeny Press

About the Author

Gloria Skurzynski was born in Dusquesne, Pennsylvania, on July 6, 1930. She and her husband Edward, an aerospace engineer, have five daughters and five grandchildren. They live in Salt Lake City, Utah.

Always a devoted reader since she received her first library card at age seven, Mrs. Skurzynski did not being writing until her youngest daughter entered first grade. She has written picture books, folk tales, middle-grade adventure stories, and novels and non-fiction for young adults. In her late teens she developed an interest in the Middle Ages. Her book *What Happened in Hamelin* was a 1979 Christopher Award winner. *Manwolf* was named a 1981 Best Book for Young Adults by the American Library Association.

Before-you-read Activities

1. Discuss the difference between a minstrel and a jester. How did a minstrel make a living? A jester?

2. Using a world map, locate the following places: France, England, The Holy Land (Palestine, Israel, Jordan, Lebanon, and Syria), and Jerusalem.

3. *Medieval Legends.* A legend is defined as a tale, or group of tales coming down from the past and usually accepted as historical despite lack of historical evidence. Using this definition, name some medieval legends. Discuss the medieval time period, roughly 1066 to 1485. Encourage the students to do some independent reading by making a display corner of some of the books from the resource section of this guide.

4. Read a version of the story of Robin Hood to the children. One is listed in the resource section at the back of this study guide. The legends about Robin Hood are set in the same time period as *The Minstrel in the Tower.* Watch the movie *The Story of Robin Hood* (1952, Walt Disney) starring Richard Todd. Have the children note the strolling minstrel that joins Robin's band.

5. Read *Francis, the Poor Man of Assisi,* written and illustrated by Tomie dePaola, (published by Holiday House) to the children. Explain that this story is not a legend but factual.

 © 1993 Progeny Press

Chapter 1

Vocabulary:

Read the sentence and define the underlined word. Look up the dictionary definition and compare.

1. Mother, Roger, and Alice waited alone in their cottage, with only their <u>elderly</u> neighbor, Zara, to visit them.

   Your definition:_____

   _____

   Dictionary definition: _____

   _____

2. When they reached the door, they stopped in <u>dismay</u>.

   Your definition:_____

   _____

   Dictionary definition: _____

   _____

3. In her lap rested a <u>lute</u>.

    Your definition:_____

    _____

    Dictionary definition: _____

    _____

4. It's <u>preying</u> on her mind.

    Your definition:_____

    _____

    Dictionary definition: _____

    _____

5. I'll sing for our suppers, like a strolling <u>minstrel</u>.

    Your definition:_____

    _____

    Dictionary definition: _____

    _____

© 1993 Progeny Press

6. "I wish I could go in your <u>stead</u>," <u>lamented</u> Zara.

<u>stead</u>
Your definition:_____

_____

Dictionary definition: _____

_____

<u>lamented</u>
Your definition:_____

_____

Dictionary definition: _____

_____

7. Her face puckered as she lifted the edge of her brown <u>wimple</u> to dab her eyes.

Your definition:_____

_____

Dictionary definition: _____

_____

Questions:

1. Alice and Roger are brother and sister. Describe their relationship. Do they get along? How do they feel about each other? _____

   _____

   _____

   _____

   _____

2. Why does Zara visit the children and their mother? _____

   _____

   _____

3. Where is the children's father?_____

   _____

   _____

4. Why was it hard for Roger to keep up with Alice?_____

   _____

   _____

© 1993 Progeny Press

5. Why does their mother ask the children to find her brother Raimond?

_____

_____

6. Why do you think Roger wanted Alice to come along? _____

_____

_____

7. Read Ephesians 6:2:

> Children obey your parents in the Lord, for this is right. "Honor your father and mother"—which is the first commandment with a promise—"that it may go well with you and that you may enjoy long life on the earth."

Roger and Alice did not know they had an uncle. Even though their mother was feverish and may have been imagining having a brother, Roger and Alice obeyed her request. What does the verse tell us? _____

_____

_____

Why is it difficult to obey like this without question? _____

_____

_____

Chapter 2

Vocabulary:

Match the word to the correct definition.

1.	___ lagged	a.	the tomb of a saint
2.	___ awed	b.	giving up one thing for another
3.	___ shrine	c.	graceful, good manners
4.	___ tatterdemalions	d.	despicable, awful
5.	___ haughty	e.	having cut off the hair
6.	___ elegant	f.	filled with reverence and admiration
7.	___ sacrifice	g.	arrogant and proud
8.	___ appalled	h.	ragged, dirty children
9.	___ wretched	i.	overcome with horror
10.	___ shorn	j.	fell behind

Questions:

1. As they travel toward Bordeaux, the children meet two pilgrims. Write 2–4 sentences explaining what this kind of pilgrim is. _____

   _____

   _____

   _____

   _____

 © 1993 Progeny Press

2. What did Roger do to get food for them? _____

   _____

   _____

3. Alice's mother calls Alice *La Guenuche*. What does *La Guenuche* mean? _____

   _____

4. What did Aurore look like? Use descriptive words in your answer. _____

   _____

   _____

   _____

5. Aurore was sacrificing her hair in an attempt to cure her father of his illness.
   Do you think she really wanted to cut off her hair? Why or why not? _____

   _____

   _____

6. Read these verses:

   "An anxious heart weighs a man down, but a kind word cheers
   him up."

   Proverbs 12:25

"Pleasant words are a honeycomb, sweet to the soul and healing to the bones."

Proverbs 16:24

What did Roger say to Aurore that was kind? _____

_____

_____

Why did it help? _____

_____

_____

© 1993 Progeny Press

Chapter 3

Vocabulary:

Define these words and use them in a sentence.

1. crossroads: _____

    _____

    Your sentence: _____

    _____

2. dense: _____

    _____

    Your sentence: _____

    _____

3. domain: _____

    _____

    Your sentence: _____

    _____

4. Crusader: _____

_____

Your sentence: _____

_____

5. visor: _____

_____

Your sentence: _____

_____

6. steed: _____

_____

Your sentence: _____

_____

Questions:

1. At the crossroads, why did Roger and Alice take the road to the left? _____

_____

_____

© 1993 Progeny Press

2. When Roger mentions their mother, Alice begins to cry. How does Roger comfort her? _____

    _____

    _____

3. Sometimes we say things we wish we hadn't. When you do, what are some things you can do or say to make the other person feel better? _____

    _____

    _____

    _____

4. What does Roger worry about as they lay in the dark before sleep? _____

    _____

    _____

5. A *simile* is a figure of speech that compares something we can imagine with something we want to describe. For example, if you want to describe your friend's coat you might say: *Her coat is as red as a cherry.* Because we know how red cherries are, we can get a better idea of the color of your friend's coat. Find and complete this simile from the book.

    Darkness dropped over the forest _____

    _____.

6. A literary technique used by many authors is the *flashback*. A flashback tells us about things that happened before the events in the story began. Sometimes this is done by having characters in the story think back and remember something that happened in the past.

    Summarize Roger's flashback. What does this tell you about him?_____

    _____

    _____

    _____

    _____

    What does Roger's flashback tell you about his father? _____

    _____

    _____

© 1993 Progeny Press

Chapter 4

Vocabulary:

Synonyms: A *synonym* is a word with the same meaning as another word. The following pairs of words are synonyms:

walk = stride
cold = chilly
neat = tidy
scarlet = red

Think of synonyms for these words:

1. ancient = _____

2. jolly = _____

3. flailed = _____

4. gallant = _____

5. barbarian = _____

6. remains = _____

7. raggedy = _____

Questions:

1. When Alice saw two people from the tower, she wanted to run and talk to them. Why did Roger stop her? _____

    _____

    _____

2. Descriptive words tell us what something looks, sounds, feels, tastes, smells, or acts like. Example: The dog was: brown, large, fast, matted, and vicious.

    On the lines below list five descriptive words for each of the two thieves the children meet.

    Simon: _____

    Odo: _____

3. How did the children get caught? _____

    _____

    _____

4. Why did Simon and Odo capture the children? _____

    _____

    _____

                              © 1993 Progeny Press

5. How did Simon react to the song Roger sang? _____

_____

_____

Chapter 5

Vocabulary:

Put the following words in alphabetical order and define them.

oath	sheer	scoffed
serf	clutch	ransom
devising	fuse	barricaded

Alphabetical Order

1. _____ Definition: _____

_____

2. _____ Definition: _____

_____

3. _____ Definition: _____

_____

4. _____ Definition: _____

_____

© 1993 Progeny Press

5. _____ Definition: _____

_____

6. _____ Definition: _____

_____

7. _____ Definition: _____

_____

8. _____ Definition: _____

_____

9. _____ Definition: _____

_____

Questions:

1. Roger and Alice heard the thieves talking outside the tower. Why have the thieves locked the children in the tower? _____

_____

_____

_____

_____

2. Why had Lady Blanche run away from her brother? _____

_____

_____

3. When Roger hears that his father is truly dead, how does he react? _____

_____

_____

4. Explain Roger's and Alice's complete plan of escape. _____

_____

_____

_____

5. Why did Roger's stomach clench as he looked at the stairs?_____

_____

_____

6. Roger climbs the stairs with Alice despite his fear of heights. Why? How does he get back down?_____

_____

_____

© 1993 Progeny Press

Dig Deeper:

7. Despite his fear, Roger did what needed to be done. Read the following Bible verses:

> "The LORD is my strength and my song; he has become my salvation."

Psalm 118:14

> "So do not fear, for I am with you; do not be dismayed, for I am your God. I will strengthen you and help you; I will uphold you with my righteous right hand."

Isaiah 41:10

> "Even though I walk through the valley of the shadow of death, I will fear no evil, for you are with me; your rod and your staff, they comfort me."

Psalm 23:4

Summarize these verses. Where does our strength come from to do what is right? _____

_____

_____

_____

Chapter 6

Vocabulary:

Circle the definition that most closely defines the word.

1.	**mocking:**	teasing	cutting	drawing	yelling
2.	**steward:**	hot dish	janitor	manager	athlete
3.	**scalawag:**	washcloth	rascal	anchor	follower
4.	**scoffed:**	choked	skipped	laughed	dropped
5.	**famished:**	faded	angry	tired	starved
6.	**warily:**	softly	untidy	nearly	carefully
7.	**stern:**	front	unsmiling	fuel	strong
8.	**urchin:**	child	fossil	bird	slave
9.	**abruptly:**	hungrily	suddenly	brokenly	loudly

© 1993 Progeny Press

Questions:

1. People were kind to Alice while she searched for two days to find Lord Raimond's chateau. How did the men at the chateau treat her? _____

   _____

   _____

2. With persistence Alice tried to explain to Lord Raimond who she was. Why was he slow to believe her? _____

   _____

   _____

3. What changed his mind? _____

   _____

   _____

4. Study the illustration of Alice and her Uncle Raimond on page 53. How do you think Alice felt in this picture? _____

   _____

   _____

5. Predict: What would have happened to Alice if she had given up? To Roger? To their mother? _____ _____

_____

_____

Dig Deeper:

6. Read Romans 5:3, 4

> . . . because we know that suffering produces perseverance; perseverance, character; and character, hope.

Why do you think this is so?_____

_____

_____

_____

_____

© 1993 Progeny Press

Chapter 7

Vocabulary:

For each of the following words, write down what you think the meaning is. Look up the dictionary definition of the word and compare it to your meaning.

1. palfrey: _____

   _____

2. ruffian: _____

   _____

3. gibbering: _____

   _____

4. loomed: _____

   _____

5. conquer: _____

   _____

Questions:

1. How did Alice and Lord Raimond find their way to the tower? _____

_____

_____

2. How did Roger trick Simon and Odo into thinking Alice was still in the tower?

_____

_____

3. What lie did Simon tell Lord Raimond? _____

_____

_____

4. As soon as Roger was free he saw the knights. What was it he thought of as soon as he looked at them? _____

_____

_____

5. Why was it so important to Roger that he climb the oak tree to get the lute?

_____

_____

© 1993 Progeny Press

Dig Deeper:

6. What are *first impressions?* _____

_____

_____

7. Describe a time when you wanted to make a good first impression on someone.

_____

_____

_____

_____

_____

_____

_____

_____

Chapter 8

Vocabulary:

Fill in the blanks with the words below that best fit each sentence.

strides   soothe

chateau   pace

shabby   heir

1. The children watched the cat _____ up and down the window sill.

2. The young man lived in a large, many-roomed _____.

3. Mother rocked the baby to _____ her.

4. The blanket was tattered and _____.

5. A prince is _____ to the throne.

6. Horses take long _____ as they begin to gallop.

© 1993 Progeny Press

Questions:

1. The very first thing Lord Raimond did was apologize to his sister Blanche. Why? _____

   _____

   _____

2. Read the following Bible verses:

   > Everyone should be quick to listen, slow to speak and slow to become angry, for man's anger does not bring about the righteous life that God desires.

   James 1:19b, 20

   > In your anger do not sin: Do not let the sun go down while you are still angry.

   Ephesians 4:26

   Lord Raimond had been angry when Lady Blanche ran away to marry her husband. If Lord Raimond had followed these verses, how would all their lives have been different? _____

   _____

   _____

   _____

   _____

3. What things make you angry? _____

    _____

    _____

    _____

    Think about the meaning of the Bible verses. According to these verses, what should you do (or not do) when you are angry? _____

    _____

    _____

    _____

4. Why did Lady Blanche cry? _____

    _____

    _____

5. How does Raimond describe Lady Blanche's husband? _____

    _____

    _____

© 1993 Progeny Press

6. Lord Raimond announces that Roger is his heir and will decide what Alice can or cannot do. What does Roger say? _____

_____

_____

7. What did Roger choose as a design for his banner? What did each thing on the banner represent? _____

_____

_____

_____

_____

Dig Deeper:

8. Read these verses about forgiveness.

   "Be kind and compassionate to one another, forgiving each other, just as in Christ God forgave you."

Ephesians 4:32

   "Bear with each other and forgive whatever grievances you may have against one another. Forgive as the Lord forgave you. And over all these virtues put on love, which binds them all together in perfect unity."

Colossians 3:13, 14

List three different examples from the book where someone shows forgiveness, kindness, or compassion. Write two or three sentences about each one. _____

_____

_____

_____

_____

_____

2. Read Romans 8:28:

    "And we know that in all things God works for the good of those who love him, who have been called according to his purpose."

    How do we see this happen in *The Minstrel in the Tower?* _____

_____

_____

_____

_____

          © 1993 Progeny Press

Word Search

Medieval Word Search:

In the left column is a short description of one of the three words listed on the right. Read the clue on the left and choose the best solution on the right. Underline the correct solution, then circle the solution words in the word search puzzle.

<u>Clue</u>   <u>Solution</u>

1. **a bard:**   boat   minstrel   knight

2. **tall structure:**   tower   spruce tree   bones

3. **opposite of serf:**   slave   Lord   beach

4. **Palestine:**   column   Holy Land   Jerusalem City

5. **mandolin:**   melancholy   lute   armor

6. **bird of prey:**   eagle   vulture   hummingbird

7. **standard or flag:**   manager   banner   underneath

8. **traveler:**   bus   pilgrim   shampoo

9. **manor:**   chateau   food   behavior

10. **administrator:**   tool   pastor   steward

11. **location of story:**   Britain   France   Ireland

12. **simian:**   smug   gypsy   monkey

```
L   H   V   S   H   D   E   L   I   S   S
M   I   N   S   T   R   E   L   T   U   L
D   S   D   R   O   L   P   E   P   A   F
R   O   N   I   W   S   W   E   I   E   R
F   I   A   G   E   A   D   T   L   T   A
A   M   L   H   R   A   H   G   G   A   N
P   M   Y   D   W   L   A   I   R   H   C
Z   S   L   U   T   E   E   C   I   C   E
X   T   O   Y   E   K   N   O   M   F   M
R   H   H   U   N   B   A   N   N   E   R
O   C   L   S   V   G   E   L   V   Q   U
P   I   O   E   V   A   D   H   X   E   Y
```

© 1993 Progeny Press

After-you-read Activities

Writing Projects:

1. Write a summary of the Crusades.

2. On page 19, Roger makes up a verse for Aurore using her name. Write a verse using your own name.

Oral Report:

Have each child prepare and give an oral report using index cards for their notes. The speech should be 5–7 minutes. Choose from the following topics:

a. Medieval Weddings   e. How a Young Man Became a Knight
b. Richard, the Lion-Hearted   f. Wandering Minstrels
c. Jousting, Pageants   g. Serfs
d. Pilgrims and Shrines   h. Other subjects of teacher's choice

Encourage students to use pictures and other visual aids.

Cooking Center:

Field Trip: In the book, Alice and Roger share bread, cheese, salted meat, and apricots with the two pilgrims. In small plastic bags (one for each child), package a small piece of bread, a slice of American cheese, a small piece of beef jerky (optional), and one or two dried apricots. If weather permits, take a long walk in the park and stop to have a picnic under a tree as Alice and Roger did.

Art Center:

1. *Design a banner.* Each child should choose the animal they want on their banner. Have children draw their design on a large piece of paper, then color or paint the finished design.

    An interesting book that may help with the design is *Design Your Own Coat of Arms, An Introduction to Heraldry* by Rosemary Chorzempa, published by Dover Publications (see resources).

2. Using the Dover publication *Life in a Medieval Castle & Village* (see resources) create a medieval frieze to put up around the room or across a bulletin board. Cut out each page and give one to each child. Provide fine-tipped markers or colored pencils.

Craft Center:

Modeling clay sculpture. Using modeling clay, let each student make a tower like the one in the story. Have the students reread the descriptions of the tower from the story to help them make a more detailed sculpture.

© 1993 Progeny Press

Additional Resources

Other books by Gloria Skurzynski:

Get the Message	(technology) grades 6 & up
Lost in the Devil's Desert	grades 6 & up
Goodbye Billy Radish	grades 2–6
Here Comes the Mail	pre-school–2nd grade
Almost the Real Thing	(simulation) grades 2–6
What Happened in Hamelin	grades 6 & up

Other Interesting Books:

The Bracken Trilogy:

The Bridge*	series by Jeri Massi, grades 3–6, published
Crown & Jewel*	by Bob Jones University Press
The Two Collars*	

The Merry Adventures of Robin Hood	by Howard Pyle, grades 4 and up.
The Adventures of King Arthur	by Angela Wilkes, grades 3–5, An Usborne Picture Classic, published by Usborne.
A String in the Harp	by Nancy Bond, grades 4–6, published by Scholastic. A Newbery Honor Book.
Harold the Herald, A Book About Heraldry	by Dana Fradon, grades 3–up to young adult, published by Dutton Children's Books.
Sir Dana: A Knight, As Told by his Trusty Armor	by Dana Fradon, grades 3–up to young adult, published by E.P. Dutton.

* A study guide for this title is available from Progeny Press.

The Book of Three	by Lloyd Alexander, grades 4–6, published by Dell.
St. George and the Dragon	by Margaret Hodges, grades 1–4, published by Little, Brown & Co.
Castle	by David Macaulay, grades 3–young adult, published by Houghton Mifflin, a Caldecott Honor Book.
Life in a Medieval Castle and Village	coloring book by John Green, grades 2–5 published by Dover.

Videos:

Castle	grades 3–young adult, based on the Caldecott Honor Book by David Macaulay, 1988 PBS Video
Francis of Assisi	1961 film starring Bradford Dillman.

© 1993 Progeny Press

Answer Key

Before-you-read Activities:

1. In the middle ages, a minstrel was a singer who sang for a living. A jester was a clown, fool, and comedian, usually in the service of a king or ruler.

Chapter 1

Vocabulary:

Students' definitions will vary.

1. older, more mature, an aged person; 2. daunted, terrified, confused; 3. a stringed musical instrument; 4. having a wearying effect; 5. a singer; 6. place or position of another; grieved, bemoaned; 7. a covering worn over a woman's head, neck, and chin.

Questions:

1. They get along well and love each other.
2. Zara helped care for their ill mother.
3. He had left years earlier to fight in the Crusades and had not returned. They did not know if he was dead or alive.
4. Alice never walked when she could run, and she never stayed on the ground when she could climb.
5. Their mother feared that she was dying and wanted their uncle to take care of them.
6. Answers will vary. He wanted her company.
7. The verse says to obey your parents and honor them. Answers will vary. It is difficult to obey unless you can trust the person you are obeying.

Chapter 2

Vocabulary:

1. j; 2. f; 3. a; 4. h; 5. g; 6. c; 7. b; 8. i; 9. d; 10. e.

Questions:

1. Answers will vary. A pilgrim was one who traveled to a holy place or a shrine. They traveled because of religious devotion, or many times because they hoped for a healing or miracle.
2. To get food, Roger sang for the woman and her daughter.
3. The monkey in skirts.
4. Answers will vary. Aurore was a lovely girl with thick, wavy, apricot-colored hair.
5. Answers will vary. Aurore's expression showed that she was sad about having to cut her hair.
6. Roger reminded Aurore that her hair would grow back. It helped because it gave her hope.

Chapter 3

Vocabulary:

1. The place where roads meet and cross.
2. Crowded together, thick, compact.
3. Someone's or something's territory.
4. A man who fought in the Crusades to win back the Holy Land.
5. The frontpiece of a helmet, usually movable, to protect the eyes.
6. A horse.

Questions:

1. Roger randomly chose the road on the right. Alice obeyed Roger, although she used the daisy to pick the road to the left.
2. He strums a tune on the lute.
3. Answers will vary.
4. He worried about whether his father was dead or alive, and if Uncle Raimond really existed.
5. like a lid on a chest.

6. Roger remembers trumpets, visors, swords, banners and shields. Each man wore a Crusader's cross on his sleeve. His father held Roger's hand as Roger cheered. Roger obviously misses his father. Roger's father waited for the very end of the column before he joined them. His father had spent as long as he could with Roger, he probably loved Roger very much. Answers will vary.

Chapter 4
Vocabulary:
1. old, antique; 2. happy, cheerful, merry; 3. beat, pounded; 4. chivalrous, polite, courteous to women; 5. an uncivilized person, savage; 6. ruins, leftovers, remnant; 7. tattered, torn, dirty.
Questions:
1. They were strangers and Roger was being cautious.
2. Answers will vary.
3. Roger jumped out to save the lute and Alice tried to save Roger.
4. The wanted to keep them as servants.
5. First his mouth dropped open in surprise, then he circled around the fire and grabbed Roger. Odo grabbed Alice.

Chapter 5
Vocabulary:
1. barricaded: obstacle, obstruction, boundary, fence.
2. clutch: grasp, grab, grip.
3. devising: scheming, planning.
4. fuse: to unite as if melted together.
5. oath: a promise.
6. ransom: saving a captive by payment of money.
7. scoffed: mock, jeer, make fun of.
8. serf: a peasant bound to the land and the lands' owner.
9. sheer: very steep, precipitous, straight down.
Questions:
1. The children are of royal lineage. The thieves hope to get ransom for the children from their uncle, who is a baron.
2. To marry a poor knight that she loved and to escape marrying a rich old count.
3. He cries.
4. Alice would go out the tiny window at the top of the tower and climb down the stone wall. Roger would imitate her voice so that Simon and Odo would not miss her and go looking for her. Alice would go find her Uncle Raimond, and bring him back to save Roger.
5. Roger is afraid of heights.
6. Roger felt that he should have been the one to go, and he had promised her. He backed down the steps on his hands and knees.
7. Our strength to do what we must, even in frightening situations, comes from God.

Chapter 6
Vocabulary:
1. teasing; 2. manager; 3. rascal; 4. laughed; 5. starved 6. carefully; 7. unsmiling; 8. child; 9. suddenly.
Questions:
1. They made fun of her and tried to catch her and throw her in the moat.
2. He didn't know his sister had children and she did not look like her mother. Answers will vary.
3. She mentioned the lute and that her mother wanted to be forgiven. Answers will vary.
4. Hopeful, happy, frightened. Answers will vary.
5. Answers will vary.
6. Answers will vary.

© 1993 Progeny Press

Chapter 7
Vocabulary:

1. A saddle horse; 2. A noisy, brutal, cruel fellow; 3. To talk and chatter on foolishly; 4. Come into view; 5. Vanquish, subdue, win.

Questions:

1. Lord Raimond whistled like a nightingale, and Roger whistled in answer to lead them to the tower.
2. Roger imitated Alice's voice. The thieves thought she was still in the tower.
3. Simon said he had his son locked up in the tower.
4. He remembered the knights his father had ridden with.
5. He had mastered his fear of heights once, now he wanted to make a good first impression on his uncle and show him that he was not afraid.
6. Answers will vary. First impressions are what you think about a person, based on your first meeting.
7. Answers will vary.

Chapter 8
Vocabulary:

1. pace; 2. chateau; 3. soothe; 4. shabby; 5. heir; 6. strides.

Questions:

1. Answers will vary. Lord Raimond wanted to make sure Lady Blanche knew how he felt.
2. Answers will vary. Most likely they would have been reunited much earlier. Roger and Alice would have been raised as the children of a noblewoman rather than as peasant children.
3. Answers will vary. If you are angry, you must not sin. You should be slow to become angry with others, and you should resolve your anger quickly.
4. She had waited for her husband to return for so long and now she knew he was dead.
5. He describes him as a good knight, a hero.
6. Roger says that Alice can climb all the trees she wants, and she can marry whomever she wants.
7. Roger chooses a nightingale to represent himself, and a monkey to represent his sister.
8. Answers will vary. Zara helps take care of Lady Blanche. Roger comforts Alice by playing the lute and singing. Aurore and her mother share their food with Roger and Alice. Lord Raimond shows kindness to Alice and rescues Roger. Lady Blanche and Lord Raimond forgive each other.

Medieval Wordsearch:

1. minstrel; 2. tower; 3. Lord; 4. Holy Land; 5. lute; 6. eagle; 7. banner; 8. pilgrim; 9. chateau; 10. steward; 11. France; 12. monkey.

```
L  H  V  S  H  D  E  L  I  S  S
M  I  N  S  T  R  E  L  T  U  L
D  S  D  R  O  L  P  E  P  A  F
R  O  N  I  W  S  W  E  I  E  R
F  I  A  G  E  A  D  T  L  T  A
A  M  L  H  R  A  H  G  G  A  N
P  M  Y  D  W  L  A  I  R  H  C
Z  S  L  U  T  E  E  C  I  C  E
X  T  O  Y  E  K  N  O  M  F  M
R  H  H  U  N  B  A  N  N  E  R
O  C  L  S  V  G  E  L  V  Q  U
P  I  O  E  V  A  D  H  X  E  Y
```